Too much of
anything is bad,
but too much good
whiskey is never
enough.

- Mark Twain

# Cheers to whisk(e)y appreciation!

Your thirst for knowledge has brought you this far. Here are some helpful tips.

### Whisk(e)y appearance:
Look at the colour. Best if you use a white background. Is it pale? Gold? Amber? In many cases, colour can indicate the age and type of cask. However, some countries allow colorants, so don't always count on this as an indicator.

### Whisk(e)y aroma:
The ideal glass to use is the Glencairn glass as it concentrates all the important aromas. Don't put your nose in the glass, it's not wine! Go ahead and sniff. Try to note what the smells remind you of and then try to pinpoint individual scents.

### Whisk(e)y tasting:
When tasting you should have it served at room temperature. Put a few drops of whisky on your tongue, let your saliva mix with it and let it disperse throughout your mouth. Take a second sip and swirl it around, slowly swallowing. Examine the texture and the aromas. You'll notice the primary flavours with the second sip. As your nasal cavity picks up the aromas it will influence the taste. Gradually take larger sips. If you feel it is too strong, try a drop or two of water. This will calm the burning alcohol effect on your senses. The water will open up different aromas and flavours as well.

Below you will find the some vocabulary to help you express the aromas. The diagram is broad so here are a few more characters you can find:

Cereal: beer, oatmeal, brioche, yeast, corn, barley, wheat, rye, cake and cookies
Floral/vegetative/herbaceous: leaves, white flowers, fresh or dry grass, mint, rose
Peat/Smoke: Burnt rubber, tar, sulfur, moss, iodine
Ocean: Seaweed, shells, salt

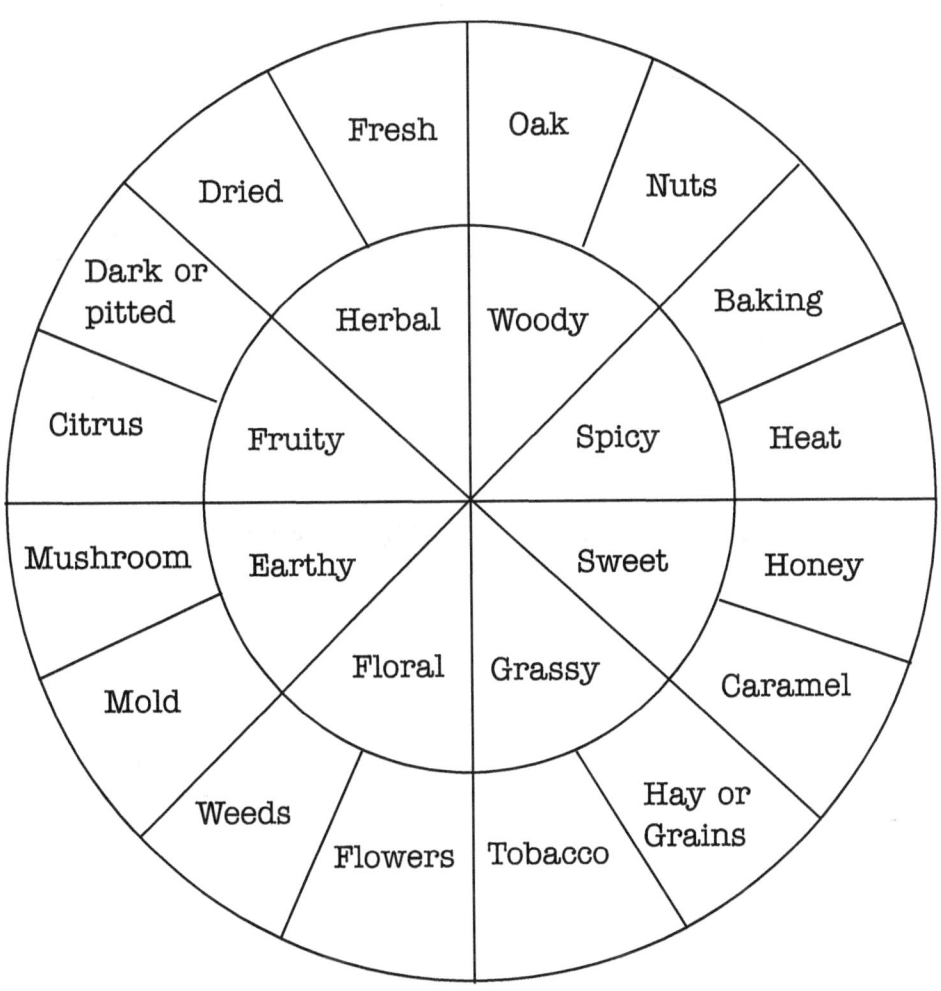

Whisk(e)y: _____

Origin: _____ %ABV: _____

Appearance:　Pale　　Gold　　Amber　　Mahogany

Viscosity:　Light　　Medium　　Heavy


Intensity: Light　　Medium　　Pronounced

Aroma:　Fruity　　Floral　　Grain　　Herb　　Spicy

　　　　　Vegetative　　Woody　　Other _____


Palate: _____

_____

_____


Finish: Simple　　Some complexity　　Very complex


Notes: _____

_____

_____

_____

Whisk(e)y: _____

Origin: _____ %ABV: _____

Appearance:   Pale   Gold   Amber   Mahogany

Viscosity:   Light   Medium   Heavy


Intensity:   Light   Medium   Pronounced

Aroma:   Fruity   Floral   Grain   Herb   Spicy

      Vegetative   Woody   Other _____


Palate: _____

_____

_____


Finish:   Simple   Some complexity   Very complex


Notes: _____

_____

_____

_____

Whisk(e)y: _____

Origin: _____ %ABV: _____

Appearance:   Pale      Gold      Amber      Mahogany

Viscosity:   Light      Medium      Heavy


Intensity:   Light      Medium      Pronounced

Aroma:   Fruity      Floral      Grain      Herb      Spicy

          Vegetative      Woody      Other _____


Palate: _____

_____

_____


Finish:   Simple      Some complexity      Very complex


Notes: _____

_____

_____

_____

Whisk(e)y: _____

Origin: _____ %ABV: _____

Appearance:  Pale   Gold   Amber   Mahogany

Viscosity:  Light   Medium   Heavy


Intensity:  Light   Medium   Pronounced

Aroma:  Fruity   Floral   Grain   Herb   Spicy

        Vegetative   Woody   Other _____


Palate: _____

_____

_____


Finish:  Simple   Some complexity   Very complex


Notes: _____

_____

_____

_____

Whisk(e)y: _____

Origin: _____ %ABV: _____

Appearance:   Pale    Gold    Amber    Mahogany

Viscosity:   Light    Medium    Heavy

Intensity:   Light    Medium    Pronounced

Aroma:   Fruity    Floral    Grain    Herb    Spicy

Vegetative    Woody    Other _____

Palate: _____

_____

_____

Finish:  Simple    Some complexity    Very complex

Notes: _____

_____

_____

_____

Whisk(e)y: _____

Origin: _____ %ABV: _____

Appearance:  Pale    Gold    Amber    Mahogany

Viscosity:  Light    Medium    Heavy


Intensity:  Light    Medium    Pronounced

Aroma:  Fruity    Floral    Grain    Herb    Spicy

    Vegetative    Woody    Other _____


Palate: _____

_____

_____


Finish:  Simple    Some complexity    Very complex


Notes: _____

_____

_____

_____

Whisk(e)y: _____

Origin: _____ %ABV: _____

Appearance:  Pale    Gold    Amber    Mahogany

Viscosity:  Light    Medium    Heavy


Intensity:  Light    Medium    Pronounced

Aroma:  Fruity    Floral    Grain    Herb    Spicy

      Vegetative    Woody    Other _____


Palate: _____

_____

_____


Finish:  Simple    Some complexity    Very complex


Notes: _____

_____

_____

_____

Whisk(e)y: _____

Origin: _____ %ABV: _____

Appearance:  Pale    Gold    Amber    Mahogany

Viscosity:  Light    Medium    Heavy


Intensity:  Light    Medium    Pronounced

Aroma:  Fruity    Floral    Grain    Herb    Spicy

        Vegetative    Woody    Other _____


Palate: _____

        _____

        _____


Finish:  Simple    Some complexity    Very complex


Notes: _____

        _____

        _____

        _____

Whisk(e)y: _____

Origin: _____ %ABV: _____

Appearance:  Pale    Gold    Amber    Mahogany

Viscosity:  Light    Medium    Heavy

Intensity:  Light    Medium    Pronounced

Aroma:  Fruity    Floral    Grain    Herb    Spicy

Vegetative    Woody    Other _____

Palate: _____

_____

_____

Finish:  Simple    Some complexity    Very complex

Notes: _____

_____

_____

_____

Whisk(e)y: _____

Origin: _____ %ABV: _____

Appearance:  Pale    Gold    Amber    Mahogany

Viscosity:  Light    Medium    Heavy


Intensity:  Light    Medium    Pronounced

Aroma:  Fruity   Floral   Grain   Herb   Spicy

      Vegetative    Woody    Other _____


Palate: _____

_____

_____


Finish:  Simple    Some complexity    Very complex


Notes: _____

_____

_____

_____

Whisk(e)y: _____

Origin: _____ %ABV: _____

Appearance:  Pale    Gold    Amber    Mahogany

Viscosity:  Light    Medium    Heavy


Intensity:  Light    Medium    Pronounced

Aroma:  Fruity    Floral    Grain    Herb    Spicy

       Vegetative    Woody    Other _____


Palate: _____

_____

_____


Finish:  Simple    Some complexity    Very complex


Notes: _____

_____

_____

_____

Whisk(e)y: _____

Origin: _____ %ABV: _____

Appearance:   Pale   Gold   Amber   Mahogany

Viscosity:   Light   Medium   Heavy


Intensity:   Light   Medium   Pronounced

Aroma:   Fruity   Floral   Grain   Herb   Spicy

   Vegetative   Woody   Other _____


Palate: _____

_____

_____


Finish:   Simple   Some complexity   Very complex


Notes: _____

_____

_____

_____

Whisk(e)y: _____

Origin: _____ %ABV: _____

Appearance:  Pale     Gold     Amber     Mahogany

Viscosity:  Light      Medium      Heavy


Intensity:  Light      Medium      Pronounced

Aroma:  Fruity    Floral    Grain    Herb    Spicy

      Vegetative      Woody      Other _____


Palate: _____

_____

_____


Finish:  Simple      Some complexity      Very complex


Notes: _____

_____

_____

_____

Whisk(e)y: _____

Origin: _____ %ABV: _____

Appearance:  Pale    Gold    Amber    Mahogany

Viscosity:  Light    Medium    Heavy


Intensity:  Light    Medium    Pronounced

Aroma:  Fruity    Floral    Grain    Herb    Spicy

      Vegetative    Woody    Other _____


Palate: _____

_____

_____


Finish:  Simple    Some complexity    Very complex


Notes: _____

_____

_____

_____

Whisk(e)y: _____

Origin: _____ %ABV: _____

Appearance:  Pale    Gold    Amber    Mahogany

Viscosity:  Light    Medium    Heavy


Intensity:  Light    Medium    Pronounced

Aroma:  Fruity    Floral    Grain    Herb    Spicy

Vegetative    Woody    Other _____


Palate: _____

_____

_____


Finish:  Simple    Some complexity    Very complex


Notes: _____

_____

_____

_____

Whisk(e)y: _____

Origin: _____ %ABV: _____

Appearance:  Pale    Gold    Amber    Mahogany

Viscosity:  Light    Medium    Heavy


Intensity:  Light    Medium    Pronounced

Aroma:  Fruity    Floral    Grain    Herb    Spicy

    Vegetative    Woody    Other _____

Palate: _____

    _____

    _____

Finish:  Simple    Some complexity    Very complex

Notes: _____

    _____

    _____

    _____

Whisk(e)y: _____

Origin: _____ %ABV: _____

Appearance:  Pale    Gold    Amber    Mahogany

Viscosity:  Light    Medium    Heavy


Intensity:  Light    Medium    Pronounced

Aroma:  Fruity    Floral    Grain    Herb    Spicy

          Vegetative    Woody    Other _____


Palate: _____

          _____

          _____


Finish:  Simple    Some complexity    Very complex


Notes: _____

          _____

          _____

          _____

Whisk(e)y: _____

Origin: _____ %ABV: _____

Appearance:  Pale    Gold    Amber    Mahogany

Viscosity:  Light    Medium    Heavy


Intensity:  Light    Medium    Pronounced

Aroma:  Fruity    Floral    Grain    Herb    Spicy

Vegetative    Woody    Other _____

Palate: _____

_____

_____

Finish:  Simple    Some complexity    Very complex

Notes: _____

_____

_____

_____

Whisk(e)y: _____

Origin: _____ %AB: _____

Appearance:  Pale    Gold    Amber    Mahogany

Viscosity:  Light    Medium    Heavy


Intensity:  Light    Medium    Pronounced

Aroma:  Fruity    Floral    Grain    Herb    Spicy

        Vegetative    Woody    Other _____


Palate: _____

_____

_____


Finish:  Simple    Some complexity    Very complex


Notes: _____

_____

_____

_____

Whisk(e)y: _____

Origin: _____ %ABV: _____

Appearance:  Pale   Gold   Amber   Mahogany

Viscosity:  Light   Medium   Heavy


Intensity:  Light   Medium   Pronounced

Aroma:  Fruity   Floral   Grain   Herb   Spicy

   Vegetative   Woody   Other _____


Palate: _____

_____

_____


Finish:  Simple   Some complexity   Very complex


Notes: _____

_____

_____

_____

www.ingramcontent.com/pod-product-compliance
Lightning Source LLC
Chambersburg PA
CBHW070300300526
45791CB00022B/1677